Unlock your serenity

Strategies and techniques on how a man master his emotion

By

Psychologist Arthur C. Robertson

Disclaimer page

The information provided in this non-fiction book is intended for general knowledge and educational purposes only. The author and publisher have made every effort to ensure the accuracy and completeness of the content presented within this book. However, they do not warrant or guarantee the accuracy, reliability, completeness, or suitability of the information provided.

Table of content

Disclaimer page

Description

Introduction

.

The science of emotion.

Here are some strategies to help you master and regulate emotions effectively.

The transformational power of mindfulness.

Here's a full description of how mindfulness may assist control our emotions:

Strategies to increase emotional intelligence and self-awareness

Here are some techniques to develop emotional intelligence and self-awareness:

Mastering your anger problems

Understanding rage problems and their **trigger**

Managing anger is vital for sustaining emotional well-being and successful relationships. Here are some ways that might help you properly handle anger:

Understanding and efficiently expressing anger healthily may bring about numerous major benefits:

Embrace courage

Conquer fear and anxiety

Techniques for lowering fear and anxiety for a daily healthy life

Tips for managing and controlling our emotions in various circumstances

Let's investigate some of these tips:
Building resilience and handling emotional issues
Practice for fostering mindfulness and emotional balance

Develop emotional intelligence in a relationship and social interaction

Understanding the relationship between cognition, emotion, and **believe**

Seeking assistance on particular emotional issues like coping with loss and conquering fear.

The reason why it is necessary to manage your emotions

What are the rewards of our emotions?

Mastering our emotions is a skill that bears several rewards in both our personal and professional life.

Emotional mastery refers to the capacity to comprehend, manage, and express our emotions healthily and productively. Here are some detailed advantages of managing our emotions:

How to build a good mentality for emotional well being

How does sleep impact our mood?

The influence of sleep on our mood

Conclusion

Description

This wonderful book" is an intriguing and instructive book that dives into the intricate and sometimes misunderstood area of emotional mastery. In this transforming book, readers are guided on an inspiring journey towards emotional intelligence and self-discovery. Drawing on years of study and personal experiences, the author gives practical tactics, cognitive techniques, and profound wisdom to help men sail the rough seas of their emotions with grace and elegance. From understanding the foundations of emotional triggers to creating effective coping techniques, this book gives men with the vital tools to grow emotional resilience and alter their lives. Through captivating real-life experiences and thought-provoking activities, readers will embark on a transforming adventure towards managing their emotions, enhancing their relationships, and attaining genuine inner balance. Whether you are seeking strategies to handle stress, conquer anger, or build a more positive outlook, "How a Man Masters His Emotions" is a must-read book for every guy who aspires to harness the power inside and lead a satisfying, emotionally empowered life. Kindly click on the "Buy Button" now to get your copy

Introduction

In the busy metropolis of New York, there lived a young guy called Ethan. He was notorious for his anger, which frequently landed him into problems and damaged his relationships. Determined to change, Ethan went on a mission to conquer his emotions.

He sought instruction from an elderly wise lady who lived on the outskirts of the city. She shared the key to emotional control with him - the power of mindfulness. She urged Ethan to become aware of his thoughts and emotions without judgment.

Ethan followed the wise woman's counsel meticulously. He began practicing meditation to calm his thoughts and acquire insight. As he got more attentive to his emotions, he learned to recognize triggers that prompted him to behave impulsively.

One day, while traveling along a busy street, someone accidentally bumped into Ethan. In the past, he would have burst into wrath, but today, he took a long breath and examined his feelings. He opted not to let the experience dictate his attitude.

Over time, Ethan noted substantial changes. He grew more patient, understanding, and sensitive toward others. He realized the power of forgiveness and learned to let go of grudges.

As Ethan managed his emotions, his relationships prospered. Friends sensed his newfound serenity and sought refuge in his company. He became a role model for others, motivating them to begin their emotional journeys.

Ethan's tale shows us that managing emotions is an ongoing journey. It involves self-awareness, patience, and the resolve to change. With effort, everyone can acquire emotional intelligence and improve their lives for the better.
Emboldened by his accomplishments, Ethan sought further ways to enhance his emotional resilience. He went into the realm of literature, psychology, and

philosophy, investigating diverse methodologies and discoveries.

Ethan learned about the power of reframing, the capacity to modify his viewpoint on hard events. When confronted with failures or disappointments, he schooled himself to perceive them as chances for progress instead of causes of irritation. This adjustment in mentality helped him to retain a feeling of optimism even in the face of hardship.

He also found the need for self-care routines to enhance his mental well-being. Regular exercise, enough sleep, and good nutrition were key aspects of his regimen. These routines not only benefited his physical health but also helped his overall emotional equilibrium.

To expand his knowledge of emotions, Ethan began participating in meaningful interactions with individuals from varied backgrounds. Through active listening and empathy, he learned to bridge gaps in knowledge and establish relationships based on common experiences and emotions.

As Ethan continued his trip, he sometimes experienced roadblocks. But instead of obsessing over his faults, he learned to accept them as stepping stones towards personal progress. He knew that emotional mastery wasn't about obtaining perfection but rather sustaining a commitment to self-improvement.

Over time, Ethan's metamorphosis was clear to those who knew him. His previously blazing rage had matured into a quiet determination, a strength created out of his newfound emotional knowledge. He became a significant person in his community, giving insight and support to those who attempted to traverse their emotional landscapes.

Ethan's experience stands as a tribute to the power of self-reflection, learning, and resilience. It shows the significant influence emotional mastery can have on our lives, relationships, and general well-being. By developing awareness, accepting change, and nourishing our inner selves, we too may begin on a similar path of emotional metamorphosis.

impacting our behavior, decision-making, relationships, and general well-being. The science of emotion strives to uncover the complicated processes behind the formation, expression, and control of emotions, giving insights into their psychological and physiological causes.

One important part of researching emotions entails identifying and comprehending the vast variety of emotions experienced by individuals. Traditionally, emotions have been categorized into fundamental categories including happiness, sorrow, anger, fear, disgust, and surprise. However, modern research reveals that emotions are more complicated and may be defined along numerous dimensions such as valence (positive or negative), arousal (intensity), and unique subjective experiences.

Neuroscience plays a significant role in uncovering the physiological foundation of emotions. Through modern brain imaging methods, researchers may pinpoint particular brain areas and neural networks related to distinct emotions. For example, the amygdala is typically linked to fear processing, whereas the prefrontal cortex is engaged in controlling and modulating emotional reactions.

Psychological theories of emotion try to explain the cognitive and evaluative processes that underlie emotional experiences. Prominent hypotheses include the James-Lange hypothesis, which posits that emotions develop as a consequence of physiological changes in the body, and the Cannon-Bard theory, which indicates that emotional experiences occur concurrently with physiological reactions.

Further understanding the social and cultural impacts on emotions is another key component of the science of emotion. Emotions are not purely individual experiences but are often impacted by social settings, cultural conventions, and interpersonal connections. Sociological study studies how emotions are impacted by social structures, societal regulations, and cultural values.

The study of emotion also explores the adaptive roles of emotions. Emotions act as information processing systems that help us navigate and respond to our surroundings successfully. They help us make choices, interact with others, and govern our behavior. For example, fear may stimulate a fight-or-flight reaction, while empathy can enhance social connection and collaboration.

Practical applications of the study of emotion have ramifications for different disciplines. In psychology and psychiatry, knowing emotions may guide therapeutic techniques for addressing mental health issues such as anxiety, depression, and trauma. In education, understanding emotional processes may lead to the creation of successful teaching practices and interventions to improve the emotional well-being of students.

The science of emotion

The science of emotion is a multidisciplinary activity that aims to explain the intricacies of human emotions. Through empirical study and theoretical frameworks, it tries to explore the psychological, physiological, social, and cultural elements of emotional experiences. Ultimately, this area of research allows a greater grasp of human behavior and leads to the creation of therapies that improve emotional well-being and psychological health.

The skills for controlling and regulating your emotions successfully

Mastering and controlling emotions successfully is vital for our general well-being and personal progress. By growing emotional intelligence, we may better manage our emotions, form stronger relationships, and face stressful circumstances with greater resilience.

Here are some strategies to help you master and regulate emotions effectively

1. Self-Awareness: Start by being more aware of your feelings. Pay attention to how you feel in various circumstances, noting the exact feelings you experience. This self-awareness helps you to spot triggers and patterns, helping you gain insight into why particular emotions develop.

2. Mindfulness and Meditation: Practicing mindfulness and meditation may provide greater clarity and peace to your mind. It helps you examine your thoughts and feelings without judgment, letting you respond rather than react hastily. Regular meditation may also strengthen your capacity to remain in the present moment, lowering tension and anxiety.

3. Emotional Regulation: Once you are conscious of your emotions, it's vital to create ways for managing them. This requires learning how to handle high emotions efficiently. Techniques like deep breathing techniques, physical activity, and gradual muscle relaxation may help you calm down and restore control.

4. **Cognitive Restructuring**: Our ideas play a crucial part in affecting our emotions. When confronted with stressful circumstances, it is crucial to analyze and fight any negative or unreasonable beliefs that may lead to emotional suffering. Replace negative ideas with more realistic and uplifting ones to modify your emotional reaction.

5. **Empathy and Perspective-Taking**: Understanding and empathizing with the feelings of others might assist in improved emotional control in social interactions. Practice active listening and attempt to view things from the perspective of others. This helps promote empathy, establish better relationships, and lessen disputes.

6. **Healthy Coping methods**: Instead of utilizing unhealthy coping methods like drug abuse or avoidance, learn better ways to deal with unpleasant emotions. Engage in things that provide you delight, such as hobbies, exercise, or spending time with

loved ones. Expressing oneself via art, writing, or talking to a trusted friend or therapist may also be useful.

7. **Emotional Boundaries**: Establishing and keeping clear emotional boundaries is vital for controlling your own emotions successfully. Understand that you are accountable for your emotions, and others are responsible for theirs. Setting appropriate limits may help avoid emotional overload and safeguard your well-being.

8. **Continuous Learning and Growth**: Emotions are complicated, and controlling them properly is a continual process. Continuously educate yourself about emotional intelligence, psychological well-being, and successful communication strategies. Attend classes, study books, or seek expert assistance to further strengthen your emotional mastery.

Remember, mastering and regulating emotions properly requires time and practice. Be patient and kind to yourself along this process. By practicing these strategies, you may build emotional equilibrium and enhance the quality of your life.

The transformational power of mindfulness

Mindfulness is an old practice that has acquired great attention and recognition in recent years, especially owing to its transforming effect. It refers to the condition of being present and aware of one's thoughts, feelings, sensations, and surroundings without judgment. This technique has been extensively accepted and implemented in different sectors, including psychology, education, and healthcare, because of its tremendous influence on people's well-being and personal progress.

One of the fundamental transforming characteristics of mindfulness resides in its potential to promote self-awareness. By fostering present-moment awareness, people become more alert to their thoughts, emotions, and physiological sensations. This heightened self-awareness helps people to notice their internal sensations without instantly responding to them, so generating a mental space for thought and decision. As a consequence, people obtain a greater knowledge of their patterns of thinking, emotional reactivity, and habitual behaviors, which allows them to make conscious choices and build healthy reactions to life's problems.

Mindfulness also supports emotional control and stress reduction. Through mindfulness activities such as focused attention on the breath, body scans, or loving-kindness meditations, people learn to create a non-judgmental and accepting attitude towards their emotions. This non-reactive position helps people to notice their feelings as fleeting phenomena rather than getting overwhelmed by them. Over time, this talent translates into enhanced emotional control, enabling people to react to difficult events with more serenity and resilience.

Moreover, mindfulness has been demonstrated to increase cognitive performance and boost mental clarity. Regular mindfulness meditation may sharpen attention, enhance focus, and boost working memory capacity. By training the mind to concentrate on the present moment, people become less distracted by rumination about the past or fears about the future. This Increased cognitive control leads to greater decision-making, problem-solving, and higher creativity.

Another transforming feature of mindfulness is its influence on interpersonal connections. By increasing present-moment awareness, people acquire deeper listening skills and become more receptive to the needs and feelings of others. This heightened empathy develops more compassionate and real interactions with people, leading to more meaningful relationships and enhanced communication.

Furthermore, mindfulness has been demonstrated to have favorable benefits on physical health. Regular practice has been connected with lower blood pressure, increased sleep quality, greater immune system functioning, and decreased symptoms of chronic pain. By lowering stress and fostering relaxation, mindfulness helps general physical well-being.

In education, mindfulness-based treatments have gained popularity as helpful tools for boosting student well-being, lowering stress, and enhancing academic achievement. Numerous studies have established the advantages of mindfulness in boosting concentration, attention, self-regulation, and emotional well-being among students. Teachers that employ mindfulness activities in their classrooms report greater student engagement, less disruptive behaviors, and better classroom atmosphere.

In essence, the transforming impact of mindfulness rests in its capacity to create self-awareness, increase emotional control, improve cognitive performance, foster meaningful interpersonal relationships, and boost physical health. By adopting mindfulness techniques into our lives, we may tap into our inner resources, build a deeper feeling of well-being, and lead more full and purposeful lives.

The benefit of mindfulness for emotional regulation
Mindfulness refers to the discipline of being completely present and engaged in the current moment, without judgment or attachment to ideas, emotions, or sensations. When it comes to emotional regulation, mindfulness has been proven to give several advantages.

Here's a full description of how mindfulness may assist control our emotions:

1. **Increased Self-Awareness**: Mindfulness cultivates self-awareness by encouraging people to examine and recognize their thoughts, emotions, and body sensations without responding to them. This heightened self-awareness provides for a better comprehension of one's emotional states and triggers, helping people to notice and treat their emotions more successfully.

2. **Emotional Recognition and Acceptance**: Through mindfulness, people learn to notice and embrace their feelings without judgment. Rather than repressing or avoiding some emotions, mindfulness fosters a loving and non-reactive approach toward them. This acceptance helps people acquire insight into the fundamental causes of their emotions and develops a healthy connection with their emotional experiences.

3. **Reduced Reactivity**: Regular mindfulness practice helps people become less reactive to their emotions. By learning to notice their emotions in a

non-judgmental manner, people may gain the capacity to stop and respond to emotional triggers rather than respond impulsively. This expanded room for reaction enables more careful and considered decisions, avoiding impulsive or damaging actions motivated by unrestrained emotions.

4. **Regulation of powerful Emotions**: Mindfulness equips people with the techniques to manage powerful emotions efficiently. By using a mindful approach, people may learn to detect the indicators of emotional escalation and practice measures to calm themselves down. These measures may include deep breathing exercises, grounding techniques, or meditation practices, all of which assist moderate the intensity and duration of powerful emotions.

5. **Increased Emotional Resilience**: Mindfulness builds emotional resilience by boosting people's capacity to negotiate and bounce back from hard emotional events. Regular practice educates the mind to be present in the face of adversity, minimizing rumination and catastrophizing tendencies. This resilience helps people to confront

25

and handle their emotions more efficiently instead of being overwhelmed or entrenched in negativity.

6. **Improved Emotional control** methods: Mindfulness strengthens people's ability to create and employ effective emotional control methods. By creating a calm and concentrated frame of mind, people may explore and experiment with numerous strategies to control their emotions. This may entail cognitive reappraisal, problem-solving, or seeking social support, all of which lead to greater emotional control.

7. **Stress Reduction:** Mindfulness has been widely related to stress reduction. By bringing awareness to the present moment, people may separate themselves from future fears or past regrets that lead to emotional dysregulation. By lowering stress, mindfulness naturally increases emotional well-being and strengthens the general capacity to control emotions successfully.

In summary, mindfulness provides a broad variety of advantages for emotional regulation through boosting self-awareness, emotional recognition, and acceptance, lowering reactivity, controlling powerful emotions, developing emotional resilience, strengthening emotional regulation tools, and reducing stress. By frequently practicing mindfulness, people may build a better and more balanced connection with their emotions, leading to increased emotional well-being and overall life satisfaction.

Strategies to increase emotional intelligence and self-awareness

Developing emotional intelligence and self-awareness is vital for personal development and increasing the quality of our relationships and interactions with others. These talents assist us to better comprehend and control our own emotions, as well as sympathize with and understand the emotions of others.

Here are some techniques to develop emotional intelligence and self-awareness:

1. **Recognize and understand your emotions**: Take the time to recognize and accept your feelings without judgment. Pay attention to the bodily sensations and ideas that develop while experiencing various emotions. Developing an awareness of the triggers that produce specific emotions might help you manage them more successfully.

2. Practice self-reflection: Set aside regular time for introspection and self-reflection. This may be done by writing, meditation, or just finding a quiet spot to ponder. Reflect on your ideas, emotions, and behaviors, and examine how these may affect your relationships with others. Self-reflection may bring awareness to patterns and behaviors that may require change.

3. Seek input: Ask trustworthy persons for comments on your conduct, communication style, and emotional responses. This may give useful insights into blind spots and places for personal improvement. Be open to hearing constructive criticism and utilize it as a chance for self-improvement.

4. Cultivate empathy: Empathy is vital for understanding and connecting with people. Practice putting yourself in other people's shoes and striving to comprehend their feelings and viewpoints. This may be done by actively listening, asking open-ended questions, and expressing genuine interest in others' experiences.

5. Develop emotional control techniques: Learn to manage and regulate your emotions in healthy ways. Identify coping tactics that work for you, such as deep breathing exercises, mindfulness, physical activity, or indulging in hobbies that offer you pleasure and relaxation. It's crucial to develop appropriate outlets for processing and expressing feelings, rather than repressing or lashing out.

6. **Enhance communication** skills: Effective communication is vital for creating healthy relationships. Practice active listening, which entails completely participating in discussions, validating others' feelings, and responding carefully. Pay attention to both verbal and nonverbal clues and try for clarity and aggressiveness in communicating your feelings and demands.

7. Seek professional assistance if needed: If you find it tough to develop emotional intelligence and self-awareness on your own, try receiving guidance from a therapist or counselor. They may give direction, resources, and approaches targeted to your unique requirements and assist you through any underlying emotional roadblocks.

8. Practice self-care: Taking care of your physical, mental, and emotional well-being is crucial. Make time for things that nourish and revitalize you, such as exercise, spending time in nature, indulging in hobbies, or practicing mindfulness. Prioritizing self-care enables you to be in a better frame of mind to build emotional intelligence and self-awareness.

Developing emotional intelligence and self-awareness is a lifetime endeavor that takes patience and regular work. By utilizing these tactics, you may progressively increase these talents and stimulate personal growth, leading to enhanced relationships, heightened self-confidence, and a higher feeling of satisfaction.

Mastering your anger problems

Mastering anger is a crucial ability that adds to our general well-being and may substantially affect our relationships, job performance, and personal progress. Anger is a normal feeling that all people experience, but it is crucial to learn how to handle it successfully rather than allowing it to rule us.

The first step in taming anger is to cultivate self-awareness. It's crucial to detect the signals that suggest we are growing upset, such as elevated heart rate, stiff muscles, or a change in our breathing rhythm. By being aware of these bodily and emotional indicators, we may start to intervene before our anger grows.

Once we are conscious of our anger, it is necessary to practice emotional management skills. Deep breathing exercises, counting to ten, or taking a break might help us calm down and gain control over our emotions. Engaging in activities such as meditation, yoga, or regular exercise may also bring long-term advantages in reducing anger by helping us create a feeling of inner serenity and emotional stability.

Another crucial component of overcoming anger is recognizing its underlying causes. Anger frequently develops from unfulfilled expectations, feelings of unfairness, or a perceived danger to our well-being. Reflecting on the factors that tend to create our anger may give significant insights into our internal thinking processes and beliefs. By confronting and reframing these underlying assumptions, we may retrain our brains to react to triggering circumstances with more reasonable and controlled emotions.

Effective communication is a critical component of anger control. Learning how to communicate our emotions assertively, rather than angrily, helps reduce the development of problems and strengthen our relationships. It entails utilizing "I" words to convey our thoughts and wants, actively listening to other's viewpoints, and finding mutually beneficial solutions. Developing empathy for others might also help us grasp their views and minimize the possibility of responding with rage.

In addition to these individual measures, getting professional aid via counseling or anger

33

management classes may be enormously useful. These materials give a safe area to investigate the fundamental reasons for anger, discover coping skills, and practice self-reflection.

Finally, it is vital to exercise self-care and stress management strategies to preserve emotional equilibrium and avoid anger from collecting. Engaging in activities we like, keeping a healthy lifestyle, and creating a support network may all contribute to our overall emotional well-being.

Mastering anger is a lifetime endeavor that needs patience, self-compassion, and a desire to learn and develop. It is crucial to remember that everyone feels anger, but how we choose to react to it is under our control. By spending time and effort into understanding and regulating our anger, we may lead more rewarding and harmonious lives, promoting healthy relationships and personal growth.

Understanding rage problems and their trigger

Anger is a complicated emotion that may be generated by numerous situations. To comprehend anger and its causes, it's vital to investigate the psychological and physiological components of this emotion.

1. Perception of danger: Anger may be aroused when a person sees a danger to their well-being, safety, or values. This danger might be genuine or imagined, and it can emanate from external sources such as disputes, criticism, or injustice.

2. Frustration: Unmet needs, desires, or expectations may lead to frustration, which can subsequently express as rage. When people are unable to fulfill their objectives or encounter frequent setbacks, they may become more agitated and prone to angry outbursts.

3. **Feelings of Injustice**: Anger may occur when someone believes they have been treated unjustly or faced a violation of their rights or principles. This might vary from personal sentiments of unfairness to seeing social injustices, resulting in a sense of moral indignation.

4. **Powerlessness and Helplessness**: When people feel powerless or helpless in a circumstance, rage may erupt as a reaction. This may happen when someone believes their autonomy or authority is challenged, resulting in emotions of wrath and irritation.

5. **Cognitive Biases**: Our beliefs and perceptions of events may impact the sense of rage. Cognitive biases such as leaping to conclusions, presuming ill motives in others, or catastrophizing might lead to the amplification of angry reactions.

6. **learned Behaviors**: Anger may also be learned via watching and copying others. If people grew up in a setting where anger was prominent or experienced violent models, they may internalize these behaviors and exhibit anger more easily.

7. Personality qualities: Certain personality qualities, such as high levels of impulsivity or poor frustration tolerance, might make people more prone to rage. These attributes may affect how a person absorbs and reacts to difficult or demanding events.

8. **Stress and Poor Coping Mechanisms**: Chronic stress or the inability to adequately deal with stress might increase the chance of feeling rage. When stress levels build up, people may have a reduced threshold for rage reactions.

It's crucial to remember that although these elements might lead to rage, everyone's triggers and reactions may differ. Understanding anger and understanding its sources may be the first step towards establishing good coping mechanisms and managing this strong emotion more successfully.

Strategies for handling rage

Managing anger is vital for sustaining emotional well-being and successful relationships. Here are some ways that might help you properly handle anger:

1. **Recognize your anger**: The first step is to be aware of your anger and accept it   judgment. Recognizing and accepting the feeling enables you to better regulate your reactions.

2. **Practice deep breathing and relaxation techniques**: When anger emerges, take the calm, deep breaths. Focus on your breath entering and exiting your body. Deep breathing helps calm your nervous system and decreases the physiological repercussions of rage.

3. **Take a timeout**: If you feel overwhelmed by anger, move away from the circumstance that generated it. Take a little pause to allow yourself time to cool down and restore perspective. Engage in things that calm you, such as listening to music or going for a stroll.

4. **Communicate assertively**: Express your anger productively and courteously. Use "I" phrases to convey your thoughts and demands without criticizing others. Avoid passive-aggressive conduct or hostile outbursts, since these might aggravate the issue.

5. **Practice empathy and perspective-taking**: Try to grasp the other person's point of view and investigate any underlying reasons for their actions. Cultivating empathy and perspective-taking may help you approach disagreements with understanding and discover more effective solutions.

6. **Find healthy outlets for anger**: Engage in activities that help release pent-up energy or fury, such as physical exercise, writing in a diary, or participating in a creative activity. Find healthy

strategies to channel your anger and release it constructively.

7. **Seek support**: If you feel that anger is frequently producing challenges in your life, consider obtaining professional treatment via therapy or counseling. A mental health expert may give advice and teach you more anger control skills targeted to your requirements.

8. **Practice self-care**: Ensure that you are taking care of your general well-being. Get adequate sleep, eat a healthy diet, exercise frequently, and indulge in things that offer you pleasure and relaxation. Taking care of oneself physically and emotionally may help lower overall stress levels and make anger management more bearable.

Remember, regulating anger is a skill that requires time and practice. Be gentle with yourself as you learn to embrace better methods of coping with this intense emotion.

The proper expression of rage is vital for our general emotional well-being and the maintenance of good relationships. While rage is typically considered a bad emotion, it serves a role in our lives.

Understanding and efficiently expressing anger healthily may bring about numerous major benefits:

1. **Emotional Release**: Anger may build up within us and badly influence our mental health if left unexpressed. Healthy expression of anger helps us to release and channel this tremendous emotion beneficially, keeping it from festering within us. When we release our anger constructively, we enjoy a sense of relief and emotional catharsis.

2. **Conflict Resolution**: Anger, when communicated responsibly, may act as a catalyst for resolving disagreements. By expressing our emotions in a controlled and courteous way, we convey our sentiments, needs, and limits to others. This helps open up a discourse, encouraging understanding and perhaps leading to problem-solving and reconciliation. Suppressing or ignoring anger, on the other hand, may intensify confrontations and delay settlement.

3. **Assertiveness and Self-Advocacy**: Expressing anger healthily develop assertiveness, which is crucial for self-advocacy and establishing boundaries. Through assertive communication, we may demand our rights, share our thoughts, and defend our needs without hostility or passive conduct. This cultivates healthy self-esteem, and self-respect, and guarantees that our views and emotions are recognized and appreciated by others.

4. Improved Relationships: Emotionally mature persons who express anger correctly tend to have happier and more rewarding relationships. By expressing anger constructively, we are more likely to be heard and understood by others, which builds empathy, mutual respect, and deeper relationships. Healthy expression of anger helps to avoid resentment or the development of unsolved concerns that may destroy relationships over time

.

5. Self-Awareness and Emotional Regulation:
Engaging in healthy expression of rage demands self-reflection and self-awareness. It enables us to uncover the underlying reasons and triggers for our anger, enabling us to better understand ourselves and

what prompts powerful emotional reactions. This self-awareness helps us to create effective coping techniques and nurture emotional regulation abilities, leading to greater control over our anger and enhanced emotional balance.

6. Stress Reduction: When anger is not addressed or is expressed inappropriately, it may contribute to chronic stress. On the other side, the appropriate expression of rage functions as a stress-release valve. By developing outlets for anger, such as productive talks, physical exercise, or creative pursuits, we may lessen the physiological and psychological repercussions of anger and prevent it from adversely harming our well-being.

In conclusion, the appropriate expression of anger is vital for sustaining emotional well-being, resolving disagreements, developing assertiveness, strengthening relationships, building self-awareness, and lowering stress. By identifying and expressing anger healthily, we may harness its strength and convert it into a beneficial force for personal development and good change.

Embrace courage

Embracing bravery is a strong activity that needs self-awareness, practice, and a willingness to venture out of your comfort zone. Here are some measures you may take to create and accept bravery in your life:

1. **Recognize your anxieties**: Courage doesn't imply the absence of fear, but rather, identifying your concerns and resolving to take action despite them. Start by recognizing the areas in your life where fear keeps you back. Self-reflection and introspection are crucial to understanding your worries.

2. **Set significant goals**: Identify what you want to accomplish or the activities you want to take that demanded bravery. These objectives should correspond with your beliefs and ambitions

Make sure they are hard enough to push you outside of your comfort zone but yet realistic enough to be doable.

3. **Break it down**: Sometimes, the notion of adopting bravery might seem overwhelming. Break

your aim or intended activity down into smaller, doable stages. This will assist build a plan and make the process less frightening.

4. **Cultivate a growth attitude**: Adopting a growth mindset is key to adopting bravery. Believe in the possibility for growth and development, recognizing that setbacks and failures are chances for learning and better. Embrace adversities as stepping stones towards personal progress.

5. **Take reasonable chances**: Courage frequently means taking risks. Assess the probable outcomes and assess whether the risks are worth incurring. Evaluate the prospective benefits and consequences and make an educated choice. Start with modest changes, gradually building up your bravery muscle.

6. **Practice self-compassion**: Remember to be gentle to yourself during this journey. Embracing bravery may be unpleasant and demanding, and setbacks are natural. Treat oneself with care, knowing that it's normal to make errors or confront hardships. Learn from them and keep going ahead.

7. **Surround yourself with support**: Seek out folks who inspire and encourage you on your road toward embracing bravery. Surrounding oneself with good and supportive individuals may give essential inspiration and confidence.

8. **Visualize success**: Use the power of imagination to see yourself successfully embracing bravery. Visualize the good consequences and how it connects with your beliefs and objectives. This may assist promote confidence and resilience.

9. **Practice mindfulness**: Cultivating mindfulness may help you remain present and focused, especially while confronting anxiety or uncertainty. Mindfulness exercises, such as deep breathing, meditation, or journaling, may help you control anxious thoughts and remain anchored in the present moment.

10. **applaud your victories**: Acknowledge and applaud your daring deeds and successes, regardless of their scale. Celebrating little triumphs can strengthen your bravery and drive you to continue embracing it in other aspects of your life.

Remember, adopting bravery is a process that demands patience and effort. As you venture beyond your comfort zone and lean into fear, you will build a better feeling of resilience, confidence, and personal development.

Conquer fear and anxiety

Conquering fear and anxiety is a multifaceted process that takes self-awareness, patience, and practice. It's crucial to remember that everyone's path is unique, and what works for one person may not work for another. That being said, here are some ideas and approaches that might be beneficial in fighting fear and anxiety:

1. **Self-awareness:** Start by recognizing and comprehending your worries and concerns. Reflect on certain triggers or events that lead you to feel anxious or afraid. This insight may help you build techniques to handle these emotions appropriately.

2. **Challenge your ideas**: Recognize that fear and anxiety are typically founded on unreasonable thinking or worst-case scenarios. When you discover yourself engaged in negative self-talk or catastrophic thinking, intentionally dispute such views by asking yourself for proof or alternate viewpoints. This may help change your perspective and minimize worry.

3. Breathing exercises and mindfulness: Deep breathing exercises may help calm your body and mind during periods of tension. Practice taking slow, deep breaths, concentrating on filling your lungs with air and gently expelling. Similarly, mindfulness exercises, such as meditation or body scanning, may help you remain present and minimize worry.

4. **Gradual exposure:** Gradual exposure to scary events or stimuli might help desensitize your fear response. Start by exposing yourself to minimally anxiety-provoking circumstances and progressively work your way up to more demanding ones. This method, known as systematic desensitization, may help you gain confidence and resilience over time.

5. **Seek help**: Don't hesitate to call out for support from trustworthy friends, family members, or experts. Consider talking to a therapist or counselor who can give direction and assistance in overcoming fear and anxiety. They may assist educate coping methods, give an outside viewpoint, and provide more resources.

6. **Take care of yourself**: Engage in self-care activities that promote relaxation and well-being.

This may involve regular exercise, appropriate sleep, good nutrition, and finding hobbies or interests that offer pleasure and satisfaction. Taking care of your physical and mental health might aid in minimizing anxiety levels.

7. **Practice stress management strategies**: Experiment with stress management techniques such as progressive muscle relaxation, guided visualization, or journaling. These strategies may help you relax, relieve tension, and achieve a feeling of control over your emotions.

8. **Set reasonable objectives**: Break down your ambitions into tiny, manageable actions. By establishing reasonable objectives and appreciating each milestone, you may increase your confidence and drive yourself to continue addressing your fears and concerns.

9. **Embrace pain**: Recognize that discomfort is a normal element of progress. Accepting that fear and anxiety may come during stressful circumstances might help you build resilience and address them head-on. Remember, it's alright to feel

uncomfortable but don't allow that to keep you back from achieving your goals and objectives

10. **Applaud progress**: Acknowledge and applaud your accomplishments, no matter how modest. Conquering fear and anxiety takes time and work, so be nice to yourself along the way. Celebrating your successes may encourage healthy habits and build your confidence for future difficulties.

Remember, mastering fear and anxiety is a personal process, and there is no one-size-fits-all method. Be patient with yourself, recognize minor successes, and seek professional assistance if required. With time and determination, you may learn to control and overcome your fears and worries, leading to a better and more fulfilled life.

Techniques for lowering fear and anxiety for a daily healthy life

Reducing the influence of fear and anxiety is vital for sustaining a healthy everyday life. Here are numerous helpful ways that might aid in controlling and conquering negative emotions
Deep Breathing and Mindfulness:

Deep breathing techniques are proven to have a soothing impact on the body and mind. By taking slow, deep breaths in and out, you trigger the body's listening, empathy, and effective expression of emotions. When we convey our ideas quietly and politely, it enhances the likelihood of finding mutually beneficial solutions, enabling emotions to be addressed and resolved productively. This increases emotional well-being by minimizing negativity, and resentment, and establishing a good emotional climate.

Moreover, communication may give emotional support during stressful situations. When confronted with problems, expressing our troubles, worries, and weaknesses with trustworthy persons helps reduce emotional burdens. By openly articulating our feelings and seeking assistance from others, we build a sense of connection, empathy, and understanding. This, in turn, may strengthen our emotional resilience, enhance our problem-solving ability, and bring comfort during difficult circumstances.

On the other hand, poor or insufficient communication has the potential to severely damage our emotional well-being. Poor communication may lead to misunderstandings, misinterpretations, and strained relationships. Not being able to express oneself freely or being misunderstood may produce dissatisfaction, bitterness, and feelings of isolation. Therefore, establishing excellent communication skills is vital in generating healthy emotional experiences and maintaining meaningful connections.

In short, communication pervades all parts of our everyday life and has a tremendous impact on our emotional well-being. By participating in good communication, we may develop and sustain meaningful relationships, communicate our feelings and needs, handle disputes constructively, and seek emotional support. These good communication habits contribute to a healthy emotional state, boost our general well-being, and establish meaningful relationships with others.

Tips for managing and controlling our emotions in various circumstances

Regulating and managing emotions is a crucial ability that may substantially affect our well-being and relationships. Emotions are a fundamental aspect of being human, yet they may occasionally become overpowering or prompt us to respond hastily. Fortunately, there are various effective ways of regulating and managing emotions in diverse settings.

Let's investigate some of these tips:

1. **Self-awareness**: The first step in managing emotions is to acquire self-awareness. Pay attention to your emotional state, recognize the exact feelings you are experiencing, and understand what generates them. This self-awareness helps you to take control of your emotions and behave more effectively.

2. **Acceptance**: Accepting and embracing your feelings without judgment is vital. Understand that feeling emotions is natural and they have a purpose. Acceptance helps in giving your emotions room and not repressing or ignoring them, which may lead to greater misery.

3. **Deep breathing and relaxation techniques**: Deep breathing exercises, such as diaphragmatic breathing, help stimulate the body's relaxation response. Regular use of these strategies may assist to decrease stress and quiet the mind, therefore facilitating good emotional control.

4. **Emotional labeling**: Give a name to the feeling you are experiencing. Research demonstrates that naming emotions may help manage them more efficiently. For example, expressing "I'm feeling anxious" or "I'm feeling frustrated" enables you to recognize and process such feelings deliberately.

5. **Cognitive restructuring**: Our ideas and interpretations profoundly affect our emotional reactions. By confronting and reframing unpleasant or unreasonable beliefs, you can manage your emotions. Replace negative ideas with more realistic

and positive ones, offering a more balanced and grounded viewpoint.

6. **Mindfulness and** meditation: Practicing mindfulness and meditation helps strengthen emotional control abilities. These activities entail observing thoughts and emotions without judgment, helping you to establish distance from them and react with more clarity.

7. **Engaging in physical** activity: Physical exercise has been demonstrated to significantly improve mood and emotional control. Engaging in sports such as jogging, walking, or doing yoga generates endorphins, which are natural mood uplifters.

8. **Seeking assistance**: Talking about your feelings with a trustworthy friend, family member, or therapist may give significant insights and support. They may give a fresh viewpoint or assist you explore alternative answers, easing the intensity of your feelings.

9. **Creating an emotional** toolbox: Develop a specific toolkit of tactics that work for you. This toolbox may include activities like writing, listening

to music, participating in hobbies, or engaging in relaxation methods. Having several approaches at your disposal helps you to pick the one that matches your present emotional state.

10. Practice self-care: Taking care of oneself is vital for emotional stability. Ensure you are prioritizing sleep, having a healthy diet, participating in activities you love, and controlling stress levels. When your total well-being is nourished, you are better able to manage tough emotions appropriately.

Remember, emotional control is a learning process that requires time and practice. Different circumstances may need different tactics, and it's vital to be patient with yourself as you learn and perfect these abilities. By applying these methods, you may establish a healthy connection with your emotions and manage varied circumstances with more ease and resilience.

Building resilience and handling emotional issues

Building resilience and efficiently addressing emotional problems is a crucial part of personal development and general well-being.

Here are various ways that might help people build resilience and successfully handle their emotional challenges:

1. Self-Awareness: Developing self-awareness is vital as it helps people perceive and comprehend their feelings. This entails paying attention to their thoughts, emotions, and responses to diverse circumstances. By being aware of their emotions, people may better recognize and solve any issues they may be encountering.

2. Emotional Intelligence: Emotional intelligence refers to the capacity to detect and control one's own emotions, as well as comprehend and sympathize with the emotions of others. Developing emotional intelligence helps people to manage emotional issues with more ease and flexibility. It incorporates abilities such as self-regulation, empathy, and effective communication.

3. good mentality: Cultivating a good mentality may considerably help resilience. This entails concentrating on the good parts of a situation and reframing negative beliefs. By maintaining an optimistic mindset, people are more likely to develop inventive solutions and bounce back from failures.

4. **Seeking help**: It is crucial to know that seeking help is not a sign of weakness, but rather a strength. Building a supporting network of friends, family, or mentors may give people emotional support, insight, and perspective through hard times. This support system might help people restore their equilibrium and give other views on their experiences.

5. **Emotion control**: Developing good emotion control abilities is vital in handling emotional issues. This entails understanding and embracing emotions without judgment, and finding healthy methods to deal with and express them. Engaging in activities

such as mindfulness, writing, or practicing relaxation methods may help people healthily control their emotions.

6. Problem-Solving and Adaptability: Resilience also entails the ability to confront difficulties and adjust to change. Developing problem-solving skills and a flexible attitude may allow people to address obstacles head-on. This involves establishing realistic objectives, reducing challenges into small stages, and being open to altering techniques as required.

7. Self-Care: Prioritizing self-care is vital for developing resilience and dealing with emotional issues. This encompasses taking care of one's physical, emotional, and mental well-being. Engaging in activities such as exercise, getting adequate sleep, eating a balanced diet, exercising hobbies, and fostering social relationships might help people maintain an optimum level of resilience.

Remember, developing resilience is a continual process that takes practice and patience. By using these tactics and integrating them into everyday life, people may strengthen their capacity to manage emotional issues and lead a more resilient and happy existence.

Practice for fostering mindfulness and emotional balance

Protruding mindfulness and emotional balance involves constant practice and commitment. Here are some successful practices:

1. **Mindful Breathing**: Set out a few minutes each day to concentrate completely on your breath. Pay attention to the feeling of breathing and exhaling, concentrating your thoughts on the current moment. This technique helps you anchor your awareness and build mindfulness.

2. **Body Scan Meditation:** Starting from the top of your head, deliberately scan your body, paying attention to any feelings or tensions you may observe. This technique helps bring awareness to your bodily and mental sensations, generating a feeling of relaxation and release.

3. Meditation and Mindfulness applications: Utilize several meditation and mindfulness applications that give guided meditation sessions and breathing exercises. These applications give systematic coaching and reminders to practice consistently.

4. Mindful Eating: Take time to thoroughly enjoy meals by paying attention to the flavor, texture, and scent of your food. Engage your senses and slow down the eating process. This technique develops increased satisfaction and appreciation for eating while cultivating attentive awareness.

5. Journaling: Write down your thoughts, emotions, and observations consistently. This exercise helps you become more aware of your emotional patterns and allows self-reflection and processing.

6. Gratitude Practice: Set aside a few minutes each day to meditate on things you are thankful for. This technique cultivates a positive mentality, changes emphasis towards good parts of life, and helps offset unpleasant feelings.

7. **Mindful Movement**: Engage in activities like yoga, tai chi, or walking meditation that stress mindful movement and physical awareness. These activities foster a feeling of anchoring and connection between the mind and body.

8. **Setting objectives**: Begin your day by setting clear objectives for how you want to come up emotionally and consciously. This practice helps you remain focused and dedicated to embodying mindfulness and emotional balance throughout your day.

Remember that constant practice is vital. Start with modest increments of time and progressively increase the length as you get more comfortable. With effort and devotion, these techniques may become an intrinsic part of your daily routine, leading to better awareness and emotional balance.

Develop emotional intelligence in a relationship and social interaction

Developing emotional intelligence is vital for developing strong, healthy, and harmonious relationships and for navigating social interactions efficiently. Emotional intelligence refers to the capacity to detect, analyze, and control our own emotions, as well as to sense and sympathize with the emotions of others. It is a skill set that helps us to successfully communicate, resolve conflict, and build meaningful relationships with people.

In relationships, emotional intelligence plays a key role. It helps people to tune into their own emotions, which is vital for self-awareness and self-regulation. When we are aware of our feelings, we can transmit them effectively to our partners, enabling open and honest communication. Effective emotional expression enables couples to settle issues more productively and enhances the emotional tie between them.

Furthermore, emotional intelligence increases empathy and understanding. It helps people to perceive and affirm the feelings of their partners, boosting emotional connection and intimacy. Empathy helps us to put ourselves in others' shoes, comprehend their viewpoints, and react with compassion and support. In partnerships, this talent provides a feeling of emotional safety and trust, establishing a stable basis for development and mutual satisfaction.

Developing emotional intelligence also benefits social interactions outside of close partnerships. It helps people manage a broad variety of social circumstances, including friendships, family relationships, and professional surroundings. Through emotional intelligence, we may successfully communicate and connect with people, building healthy and lasting connections.

Emotional intelligence also benefits dispute resolution. By improving self-awareness and emotional control, people may calm themselves in the middle of a debate, enabling them to reply logically instead of responding impulsively. Additionally, emotional intelligence helps people de-escalate uncomfortable situations by empathizing with the feelings of others and finding mutually beneficial solutions.

Moreover, emotional intelligence plays a key role in leadership and cooperation. Leaders with high emotional intelligence can successfully understand and manage the emotions of their team members, providing a healthy and supportive work environment. They may inspire and encourage their staff, boosting teamwork and production. Similarly, emotional intelligence helps team members to operate well together, boosting collaboration and communication.

Building emotional intelligence is vital for effective relationships and social interactions. It lets people handle disputes, communicate successfully, develop meaningful relationships, and sympathize with others around them. By strengthening these talents, we may promote healthier, happier, and more rewarding relationships, as well as create good good and supportive social settings.

Understanding the relationship between cognition, emotion, and belief

The relationship between cognition, emotion, and belief is a complex and interconnected process that plays a key role in defining our vision of the world and affecting our actions and behaviors. To realize this link, it is vital to investigate each aspect independently and then understand how they interact with one another.

Thought refers to the mental processes involved in thinking, analyzing, and generating ideas, views, and judgments. Our ideas are the consequence of cognitive processes such as perception, memory, attention, and reasoning. They are impacted by a range of variables, including our prior experiences, cultural background, education, and personal prejudices. Thoughts may be conscious or unconscious and vary from instinctive, brief ones to intentional and thoughtful ones.

Emotion, on the other hand, covers our subjective experiences and responses to internal and external stimuli. Emotions are complex psychological and physiological reactions that are often defined by sensations such as happiness, anger, fear, sorrow, and joy. Emotions come from the perception of events, circumstances, or ideas, and they may have a substantial influence on our psychological and physical well-being. Emotions may be powerful or subtle, and they typically inspire action or behavior.

Beliefs are the deeply established assumptions, views, or convictions that we have about ourselves, others, and the world around us. They typically operate as filters via which we interpret and make meaning of our experiences. Beliefs may be shaped by several variables, including cultural, religious, and social influences, as well as personal experiences and education. Our beliefs affect our ideas and feelings, and conversely, our thoughts and emotions may support or challenge our previous beliefs.

The link between thinking, emotion, and belief is reciprocal and dynamic. Our ideas produce emotions, and these feelings, in turn, may impact our thoughts and beliefs. For example, if we regularly think poorly about our talents, we are likely to feel emotions such as self-doubt, fear, or melancholy, which may further develop the notion that we are not competent or deserving. On the other side, positive ideas may give birth to feelings such as confidence, happiness, or optimism, supporting the belief in our talents and potential

Moreover, our beliefs may impact our thoughts and emotions by functioning as filters. If we have a notion that individuals are typically untrustworthy, we may take ambiguous events as reinforcement of this idea, leading to unpleasant thoughts and feelings such as mistrust or anxiety. Alternatively, if we have a belief in the intrinsic goodness of others, we may read comparable events with greater trust and optimism, generating positive thoughts and feelings.

It is crucial to remember that the link between thinking, emotion, and belief is neither permanent nor unchanging. It may be impacted and transformed by self-reflection, cognitive restructuring, treatments, and fresh experiences that challenge our prior ideas. By being conscious of our thoughts, feelings, and beliefs, and actively working on them, we may promote healthier and more adaptable patterns that increase our well-being and personal progress.

In conclusion, thinking, emotion, and belief are closely intertwined and impact one another in a constant feedback loop. They affect our beliefs, actions, and behaviors and play a critical part in our overall psychological functioning. Understanding and examining the link between these factors may give vital insights into our thinking processes, emotional experiences, and underlying beliefs, helping us to grow better self-awareness and personal development.

Seeking assistance on particular emotional issues like coping with loss and conquering fear.

Seeking advice in particular on emotional concerns may be immensely useful when it comes to dealing with loss or conquering anxiety. These are two profoundly personal and complicated feelings that may be overpowering and tough to handle on our own. However, with the correct direction and support, it is possible to go through these feelings and find healing and progress.

When it comes to grieving, the death of a loved one or a huge life event may rock us to our core. It is fairly unusual to feel a broad variety of emotions such as grief, rage, guilt, or even apathy. Seeking help in such instances enables us to handle our emotions in a healthy and useful way. A grief counselor or therapist may give us a safe environment to express our emotions, examine the meaning of our loss, and help us create coping mechanisms to navigate through the grieving process. They may give insights into the intricacies of grieving, normalize our feelings, and help us discover ways to respect the memory of our loved ones while moving ahead in our lives.

Overcoming fear is another area where seeking help may be incredibly useful. Fear may emerge in numerous ways, such as phobias, anxiety disorders, or general worries that hold us back from following our goals and objectives. Working with a therapist or a coach who specializes in fear and anxiety may give us skills and methods to address and conquer our anxieties. They may help us uncover the fundamental reasons for our anxieties, challenge negative thinking patterns, and aid us in progressively facing our fears in a supportive and regulated way. By breaking down our concerns into manageable stages, we may gradually build resilience and grow the courage to tackle them.

In both sorrow and terror, seeking assistance provides several advantages beyond the knowledge of specialists. It gives a non-judgmental environment for us to discuss our experiences, ideas, and emotions, which may be wonderfully relieving. Guidance may also give essential viewpoints and ideas that we would not have explored on our own. Sometimes, just having someone listen carefully and affirm our feelings may be very soothing and deeply therapeutic.

It is vital to highlight that asking for assistance does not suggest weakness; rather, it is a show of strength and a proactive move toward personal progress and well-being. We all confront emotional issues at various stages in our life, and having the humility to seek help demonstrates a want to learn, develop, and heal.

When seeking counseling, it is crucial to identify a professional that specializes in the exact emotional difficulty you are suffering, whether it be sorrow or fear. Look for qualified therapists, counselors, or coaches with experience and skill in the area you need help with. Additionally, try obtaining help from support groups or community organizations that specialize in the emotional difficulty you are struggling with. Connecting with individuals who have gone through similar circumstances might bring further comfort and understanding.

seeking assistance in particular emotional challenges like managing loss or conquering fear may give us the support, resources, and insights required to traverse these complicated emotions. It is a daring step towards healing, progress, and finding a revitalized sense of purpose and well-being. Remember, you do not have to tackle these emotional issues alone; there are specialists and support networks available to aid you on your path.

The reason why it is necessary to manage your emotions

Mastering your emotions is vital for personal development, well-being, and general success in life. Emotions have a vital influence on our everyday experiences, relationships with others, decision-making, and overall mental and physical health. Here are numerous reasons why it is crucial to manage your emotions:

1. **Emotional intelligence**: Mastering your emotions boosts your emotional intelligence. Emotional intelligence is the capacity to detect, comprehend, and manage your own emotions as well as sympathize with and navigate the emotions of others. It helps you establish strong interpersonal connections, excellent communication skills, and a greater awareness of yourself and others.

2. **Improved self-awareness**: By managing your emotions, you achieve a better degree of self-awareness. You become more alert to your thoughts, emotions, and behaviors, helping you to

comprehend the fundamental reasons behind your emotional states. This self-awareness helps you to better regulate and control your emotions, preventing them from adversely affecting your actions and choices.

3. Stress management: Emotions and stress are strongly related. When you control your emotions, you develop the capacity to properly manage and deal with stress in healthy ways. Instead of being overwhelmed by stress, you may react with resilience, retaining a calm and collected frame of mind. This decreases the detrimental effect of stress on your mental and physical well-being.

4. Enhanced decision-making: Emotions may confuse cognition and lead to hasty decision-making. When you achieve command of your emotions, you can think more sensibly and critically in times of stress or powerful emotions. This helps you to make better-informed judgments, considering both the cognitive elements and the emotional ramifications of your choices.

5. Positive relationships: Emotions profoundly impact our connections with others. When you manage your emotions, you have better control over your reactions and responses, guaranteeing healthier and more productive communication. You become more able to manage disputes, negotiate hard discussions, and approach relationships with empathy and understanding.

6. **Increased resilience**: Life is filled with ups and downs, and managing your emotions equips you with the resilience required to navigate through hard situations. Instead of being overwhelmed by negative emotions, you may nurture a positive mentality, adapt to adversity, and bounce back from setbacks more efficiently.

7. **Mental and physical well-being**: Suppressing or ignoring emotions may significantly affect your mental and physical health. Mastering your emotions helps you to recognize, analyze, and healthily express your emotions. This adds to higher general well-being, lowering the risk of mental disorders, increasing sleep quality, and promoting overall life satisfaction.

In essence, understanding your emotions is vital for personal development, successful relationships, effective decision-making, stress management, and general well-being. It helps you to understand yourself and others better, handle stress in healthy ways, make educated decisions, and generate good and satisfying experiences in life.

What are the rewards of controlling our emotions?

Mastering our emotions is a skill that bears several rewards in both our personal and professional life. Emotional mastery refers to the capacity to comprehend, manage, and express our emotions healthily and productively. Here are some detailed advantages of managing our emotions:

1.**better Mental Well-being**: When we can properly control and regulate our emotions, we enjoy better mental well-being. We grow more resilient in the face of obstacles, stress, and adversity. This permits us to retain an optimistic outlook, deal with challenging circumstances, and bounce back from setbacks more rapidly. As a consequence, our entire mental health and emotional stability are boosted.

2. **Enhanced Relationships**: Emotional intelligence plays a critical role in creating and fostering meaningful relationships. When we conquer our emotions, we become more sympathetic, understanding, and compassionate toward others. We gain superior communication skills since we can

communicate ourselves calmly and assertively without allowing our emotions to overcome us. This leads to better and more meaningful interactions with friends, family, coworkers, and love partners.

3. Effective Decision-making: Emotions have a huge influence on our decision-making process. When we are overcome by powerful emotions such as wrath or fear, our judgment might get confused, leading to hasty and foolish actions. However, when we have emotional mastery, we are more prepared to disengage from our emotions and think logically. We may examine circumstances objectively, consider many viewpoints, and make educated decisions based on logic and reason rather than being simply influenced by our emotions.

4. Increased Resilience: Life is full of ups and downs, and managing our emotions helps us become more robust in coping with these problems. Instead of being dominated by negative feelings, we should regard setbacks as chances for development and learning. By keeping a positive and collected mentality, we can adapt to change, bounce back from setbacks, and persist in the face of adversity.

This resilience permits us to maneuver through life's uncertainties with more ease and strength.

5. **Improved Conflict Resolution**: Conflict is a normal component of human interactions, but how we manage it may decide the result. When we have emotional mastery, we are more suited to handle disagreements productively. We may approach arguments with a calm and open mentality, actively listen to others, and voice our ideas without getting defensive or confrontational. This enables more effective problem-solving, cooperation, and the ability to establish deeper and healthier connections.

6. **Increased Self-awareness**: Mastering our emotions demands self-awareness since it entails knowing our emotional triggers, patterns, and how our emotions affect our ideas and actions. By growing this self-awareness, we obtain a greater knowledge of ourselves and our emotional needs. This allows us to make conscious decisions and take proactive measures toward self-improvement, personal development, and living a more satisfying life.

In conclusion, managing our emotions delivers an assortment of advantages that favorably influence our well-being, relationships, decision-making, resilience, conflict resolution, and self-awareness. By increasing emotional intelligence, we may navigate through life with more ease, and aim for personal and professional success.

It helps you to face obstacles, setbacks, and disagreements with calm and resilience while maintaining strong connections with coworkers, clients, and superiors. Effective emotional control also boosts your problem-solving skills, flexibility, and leadership talents, making you a valuable asset in the workplace and improving the probability of job progression.

6. Personal development and fulfillment: Mastering your emotions is a vital aspect of personal growth and self-improvement. It enables you to become more in sync with your values, objectives, and desires. By managing your emotions, you may pursue objectives with more commitment, conquer hurdles with perseverance, and retain a positive view in the face of hardship. Ultimately, managing your emotions leads to a feeling of contentment, as you become more connected with your genuine self and enjoy more emotional well-being.

Conquering your emotions is not about suppressing or dismissing them, but rather about understanding, regulating, and expressing them healthily and helpfully. It helps you to face life's obstacles with resilience, make wise choices, foster meaningful relationships, and achieve personal and professional success. By investing in emotional mastery, you start on a transforming path of self-discovery, development, and well-being.

How to build a good mentality for emotional well being

Cultivating a good mentality and emotional well-being is vital for living a full and joyful life. While it may take time and effort to cultivate these skills, the advantages are well worth it. Here are some tactics you may apply to create a happy mentality and emotional well-being:

1. Practice self-awareness: Start by being aware of your thoughts, feelings, and emotions. Pay attention to the patterns of negative thinking or self-criticism that may be holding you back. Recognize that you can choose how you view and react to things.

2. Develop resilience: Life is full of ups and downs, and creating resilience helps you to bounce back from setbacks. Embrace failure as a chance for progress and regard setbacks as transitory hurdles that can be overcome. Focus on your strengths and the progress you have made rather than concentrating on faults.

3. Seek support: Surround yourself with positive and supportive folks who boost you. Reach out to friends, relatives, or a therapist when you need to chat or seek help. Having a solid support system may bring crucial views and comfort during challenging situations.

4. **self-care practice**: be responsible of your physical, mental, and emotional well-being. Prioritize things that offer you pleasure and relaxation, such as exercise, meditation, pursuing hobbies, or spending quality time with loved ones. Set appropriate limits and create time for self-reflection and renewal.

5. Practice thankfulness: Cultivate a feeling of appreciation by consistently noticing and appreciating the good parts of your life. Make a practice of writing down or verbalizing things you are thankful for each day. This technique helps shift your emphasis towards the positive and fosters a more optimistic mindset.

6. confront negative ideas: When negative thoughts come, confront them by questioning their reality. Look for evidence that supports or contradicts these views. Replace negative self-talk with positive affirmations and realistic ideas. Cognitive restructuring treatments, such as cognitive-behavioral therapy, may be useful in this process.

7. Engage in mindfulness: Mindfulness entails being present in the moment without judgment. Practice attentive breathing, meditation, or participate in activities that bring you into the present moment, such as yoga or strolling in nature. Engaging in mindfulness helps decrease stress, develop self-awareness, and promote emotional well-being.

8. **Set significant objectives**: Having clear goals and a feeling of purpose provides your life direction and inspiration. Set reasonable and attainable objectives that correspond with your beliefs and interests. Break things down into tiny stages to make them more doable and celebrate each milestone along the way.

9. Practice empathy and compassion: Treating people with empathy and kindness not only helps them but also adds to your emotional well-being.

Engage in acts of compassion, volunteer, or support people in need. These behaviors establish healthy relationships and develop sentiments of contentment and compassion.

10. Limit exposure to negativity: Limit your exposure to negative influences such as excessive media intake, unhealthy relationships, or settings that bring you down. Surround yourself with positive influences, uplifting material, and surroundings that encourage your well-being.

Remember, building a healthy mentality and emotional well-being is a lifetime endeavor. Be gentle with yourself and allow for self-compassion as you navigate through problems. By adopting these tactics regularly, you may create a positive mentality and emotional well-being, leading to a happier, more satisfying existence.

How does sleep impact our mood?

Sleep has a key function in managing our general mood and emotional well-being. The amount and quality of sleep we obtain may dramatically affect our emotional states. There are various ways in which sleep affects our mood:

1. **Emotional Regulation**: Adequate sleep promotes improved emotional regulation, helping us to deal with everyday challenges more efficiently. When we are well-rested, our brain is better suited to manage emotional difficulties and control our emotions and responses. On the other hand, sleep deprivation hinders our emotional control, making us more prone to experience mood swings, impatience, and impulsive conduct.

2. **Neurotransmitter Balance**: Sleep helps maintain a healthy balance of neurotransmitters in our brain. Neurotransmitters including serotonin, dopamine, and norepinephrine play key roles in regulating mood and emotions. Sufficient sleep ensures that these neurotransmitters are generated and

functioning efficiently, encouraging an enhanced mood and general emotional well-being.

3. **Stress Reduction**: Sleep plays a significant function in stress reduction. When we sleep, our body and mind have a chance to recuperate and regenerate, lessening the detrimental influence of stress on our mood. Sleep deprivation, on the other hand, raises stress levels, making us more prone to mood disorders and diminishing our capacity to deal with stress efficiently.

4. **Cognitive performance**: Sleep and mood are strongly interwoven with cognitive performance. Sufficient sleep promotes optimum cognitive function, including memory, concentration, and decision-making. When we lack sleep, these cognitive processes are disrupted, severely influencing our mood and emotional stability.

5. **Hormonal Balance**: Sleep impacts the synthesis and control of several hormones that affect our mood. Lack of sleep may disturb the balance of hormones such as cortisol (the stress hormone) and melatonin (the sleep hormone), leading to higher stress levels and impaired mood stability.

6. **Mental Health**: Chronic sleep deprivation has also been related to an increased risk of acquiring mental health issues including depression and anxiety. Sleep disruptions are commonly connected with the beginning and worsening of these diseases, showing the tight association between sleep and mood disorders.

Sleep deprivation or poor sleep quality may have significant consequences on our mood and emotional well-being. On the other hand, prioritizing and keeping regular sleep patterns may dramatically enhance our mood control, emotional stability, and general mental health. It is crucial to ensure we obtain adequate high-quality sleep to sustain a happy mood and emotional balance in our everyday life.

The influence of sleep on our mood

Sleep has a huge influence on our mood. Adequate and good-quality sleep is vital for sustaining emotional well-being and managing our emotions. When we don't get enough sleep or have poor sleep quality, it may have a detrimental influence on our mood, leading to irritation, mood swings, and an overall negative perspective.

During sleep, our brain analyzes emotions and consolidates memories, helping to manage our emotional reactions. Lack of sleep disturbs these processes, resulting in difficulty in controlling emotions appropriately. This may show greater irritation, less patience, and heightened sensitivity to stress.

Additionally, sleep loss may also interfere with the synthesis of chemicals that influence mood, such as serotonin and dopamine. When these hormones are unbalanced, it might lead to feelings of anxiety, despair, and general mood problems.

Furthermore, lack of sleep may impede cognitive function, making it difficult to focus, solve issues, and control emotions efficiently. This cognitive impairment contributes to the negative influence on mood, as it becomes tougher to deal with everyday pressures and keep a happy mentality.

On the other side, receiving adequate and high-quality sleep promotes higher emotional well-being. It enables emotional modulation, boosts resistance to stress, and helps maintain a happy mood. When we sleep well, we are more likely to have a stable and balanced emotional state, increased cognitive performance, and a stronger capacity to deal with adversities.

To maximize mood via sleep, it is necessary to emphasize proper sleep habits. Establishing a regular sleep schedule, having a pleasant sleep environment, practicing relaxation methods before bed, and avoiding stimulants like coffee or electronic devices close to bedtime are some beneficial ways. By prioritizing sleep and ensuring we receive adequate restful sleep, we may favorably improve our mood and general emotional well-being.

Conclusion

In conclusion, managing our emotions is a vital component of creating a good and satisfying existence. Emotions, while frequently surprising and strong, have a tremendous influence on our general well-being. By recognizing and skillfully controlling our emotional reactions, we may manage life's obstacles with grace and perseverance.

To begin this path, it is necessary to acquire self-awareness. By consciously listening to our emotions, we may recognize their causes and patterns. This awareness permits us to respond, rather than react, to events. With effort and patience, we may acquire emotional intelligence, which helps us to understand ourselves and others on a deeper level.

Furthermore, it is crucial to realize that emotions are a normal and necessary component of being human. Rather than hiding or rejecting them, we should embrace and accept them. By providing ourselves with permission to feel, we make room for healing and development.

Effective practices such as mindfulness, meditation, and deep breathing techniques are great tools for managing our emotions. These routines assist bring us into the present moment, relaxing our brains and helping us to behave sensibly rather than impulsively.

Additionally, developing a solid support system plays a key role in emotional well-being. Surrounding oneself with good, uplifting folks who give empathy and understanding develops an atmosphere favorable to emotional development

Lastly, prioritizing self-care is vital. Engaging in things that offer us pleasure, following healthy behaviors such as regular exercise, and keeping a balanced lifestyle all contribute to emotional stability.

By managing our emotions, we unleash the possibility of a better, happier existence. We develop the capacity to face problems with perseverance, create good connections, and cultivate a feeling of serenity and happiness inside ourselves. Remember, it is not about removing emotions but rather learning to harness their power, eventually developing a meaningful and emotionally balanced living.

www.ingramcontent.com/pod-product-compliance
Lightning Source LLC
Chambersburg PA
CBHW062351290526
45794CB00005B/2178